Enchanting
Creatures

Camilla de la Bédoyère

Quarto is the authority on a wide range of topics.

Quarto educates, entertains and enriches the lives of our readers—enthusiasts and lovers of hands-on living.

www.quartoknows.com

Author: Camilla de la Bédoyère
Editor: Emily Pither
Designer: Dave Ball

First Published in 2019 by QEB Publishing,
an imprint of The Quarto Group.
6 Orchard Road
Suite 100
Lake Forest, CA 92630
T: +1 949 380 7510
F: +1 949 380 7575
www.QuartoKnows.com

A CIP record for this book is available from the Library of Congress.

ISBN 978-0-7112-4560-0

Manufactured in Guangdong, China TT062019

9 8 7 6 5 4 3 2 1

MIX
Paper from responsible sources
FSC® C016973
FSC
www.fsc.org

Contents

Enchanted to Meet You!

Are you ready to be charmed by some of the most enchanting creatures in the world?

From the hummingbird, to the glasswing butterfly, these curious creatures seem magical but are in fact real! Some animals have beautiful feathers, while others change color. Some flutter or dance, and others even grow limbs! It's time to discover more about these amazing creatures.

The Enchanting Stats contain details about the location, color, size, characteristics, and "enchanting factor" of each creature.

Enchanting Stats

Location	America
Color	Green, white, and purple
Size	Small
???	Lays two eggs in a tiny nest
★★★	5/5

Weedy Seadragon

Did you know there are dragons in the crystal-blue seas?

Enchanting Stats

Location	Australia
Color	Red, yellow, and purple
Size	Small
???	Fathers look after baby seadragons
★★★	3/5

6

Seadragons are frilly fish that dance through meadows of sea grass. They move very slowly, sucking up food with their long snouts. Seadragons love to play hide and seek. They are almost impossible to see in seaweed!

Narwhal

Some people call narwhals unicorns of the sea!

Enchanting Stats

Location	Arctic Ocean
Color	Black, gray, and white
Size	Large
???	Only male narwhals usually grow a tusk
⭐⭐⭐	2/5

The long curly tooth of a narwhal looks like a unicorn's horn. This strange tooth is called a tusk and no one knows why a narwhal needs it. Maybe it can do magical things, like help the whale to find food in the chilly seas where it lives.

Starfish

You can see stars in the ocean as well as the sky...

Enchanting Stats

Location	Shallow seas worldwide
Color	Many colors
Size	Small
???	Some starfish can regrow arms
⭐⭐⭐	3/5

Colorful starfish look like magical charms that have been swept up onto a golden beach. These strange little animals use their arms to slowly creep along the seabed. When you see one, make a wish, and maybe your dreams will come true!

Glasswing Butterfly

Watch this tiny fairy fluttering by...
and see it disappear!

Enchanting Stats

Location	Central and South America
Color	Transparent wings with black or orange
Size	Small
???	Can use their feet to taste food
⭐⭐⭐	4/5

12

The glasswing butterfly can perform a special magic trick—it can vanish in a second. Its wings are see-through, so when it settles for a rest on a leaf or colorful flower it becomes invisible.

Bird of Paradise

This bird dips, dives, and dances like a dainty woodland fairy.

Enchanting Stats

Location	Papua New Guinea
Color	Many colors
Size	Small
	Male birds dance to impress female birds
	4/5

14

As he moves, this dazzling bird shakes his beautiful long feathers and brings light and color to his home. In some legends birds of paradise are the magical spirits of people who once lived in the deep, dark forest.

Peacock

This is the king of birds and he wears a crown of blue-tipped feathers.

Enchanting Stats

Location	India and Sri Lanka
Color	Blues and greens
Size	Medium
???	Peacocks sleep in trees at night
⭐⭐⭐	5/5

Peacocks have long colorful tail feathers that they drag behind them, like the train of a beautiful robe. Suddenly, the bird raises his tail to make a shimmering fan that is decorated with sparkling "eyes." Some peacocks are white, with long, dazzling feathers.

Chameleon

Chameleons are lizards that can change color—it's magic!

Enchanting Stats

Location	Africa
Color	Many colors
Size	Small
???	Catches bugs with a sticky tongue
⭐⭐⭐	3/5

18

When a chameleon is hiding in the rainforest it is green or brown because those colors are perfect for being invisible. But when it gets scared, angry, or excited it changes color. Chameleons can start to turn bright red, pink, or yellow in the blink of an eye!

Pink River Dolphin

Do you believe that dolphins can change into people?

Enchanting Stats

Location	South America
Color	Pink
Size	Large
???	They make clicking noises to chat to each other.
⭐⭐⭐	2/5

This enchanting creature is a pink river dolphin and it lives in the Amazon River. Long ago, people told stories of river dolphins changing into humans at night, and stepping onto the land. As the sun rose in the morning, they returned to the river and the life of a dolphin.

21

Axolotl

The sun goes down and this astonishing axolotl comes out to play!

Enchanting Stats

Location	Mexico
Color	Black, white, pink, or yellow
Size	Small
???	These cute amphibians are rare
★★★	3/5

22

Wild axolotls live in lakes in Mexico and they use the feathery frills on their head to breathe underwater. Axolotls can perform an amazing trick if they lose a leg—they can magically grow a new one!

Markhor

This brave beast with incredible horns is fearless and strong.

Enchanting Stats

Location	Asia
Color	Red-brown, gray
Size	Medium
???	Fur turns gray in the winter
★★★	2/5

Markhors are wild goats that live on mountains. They have long beards and use their long, spiral horns to fight each other. Long ago, people believed that markhors protected them from evil snakes, but now they are loved simply for their courage and beauty.

Crowned Crane

When a crane is in love it likes to do a delightful dance!

Enchanting Stats

Location	East Africa
Color	White, black, or gray
Size	Medium
???	There are 15 types of crane
★★★	4/5

These cranes are wearing crowns of colored feathers on their heads, and they move with the grace and elegance of a ballerina. Sometimes whole flocks of cranes dance together, leaping into the air with their wings spread out wide.

Snowy Owl

Owls often appear in fairy tales and stories of magical creatures.

Enchanting Stats

Location	Arctic
Color	White, gray
Size	Medium
???	Their large eyes help them see in the dark
⭐⭐⭐	5/5

Snowy owls have a ghostly call, large eyes, and fluffy white feathers. They live in cold places where winters are long and dark, and snow and ice cover the ground. Owls are often believed to be wise and helpful birds.

Blue Sea Dragon

This strange creature has a spellbinding secret!

Enchanting Stats

Location	Oceans worldwide
Color	Blue
Size	Tiny
???	Also called the blue angel
★★★	4/5

Dragons breathe fire, but this blue sea dragon has scary stings instead. It floats on the surface of the sea, where its silvery-blue skin shimmers in the sunlight. If it bumps into something tasty or scary it uses its stingers to slay its prey!

31

Blue Morpho Butterfly

This creature may look like a sparkly fairy, but it's actually a butterfly!

Enchanting Stats

Location	Mexico and South America
Color	Blue
Size	Small
???	Often fly near rivers
⭐⭐⭐	4/5

32

As light pours through the rainforest trees, the Sun's golden rays catch the bedazzling wings of a blue morpho. It flutters by, and the shiny scales on the butterfly's wings scatter the light, creating blue flashes that sparkle and glitter.

Hummingbird

This is a precious jewel of a bird that hums as it flies!

Enchanting Stats

Location	America
Color	Green, white, and purple
Size	Small
???	Lays two eggs in a tiny nest
★★★	5/5

34

Hummingbirds are the smallest birds in the world. They flap their tiny wings so fast they make a humming sound as they sup sweet nectar from flowers. Hummingbirds are often mistaken for fairies when they visit gardens.

Splendid fairy Wren

Lots of these little fairies live together in friendly families.

Enchanting Stats

Location	Australia
Color	Blue
Size	Small
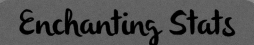	Females are brown all year
★★★	3/5

When streaks of blue flash past you, you can pretend you've been sprinkled with fairy dust. Males turn a brilliant azure blue when they want to attract a mate, but—like magic—they turn brown for the rest of the year!

Seahorse

This magical sea creature will cast its spell on you!

Enchanting Stats

Location	Shallow seas worldwide
Color	Many colors
Size	Small
???	Many seahorses can change their color
★★★	3/5

Long ago, people believed that seahorses grew so big and strong they could carry mermaids, who would ride them under the sea. Real seahorses are a type of small fish that cannot swim very well. They wrap their curly tails around seaweed and coral so they don't float away.

Spirit Bear

This bewitching bear is said to have magical powers.

Enchanting Stats

Location	Canada
Color	White or cream
Size	Large
???	Also called Kermode bears
★★★	4/5

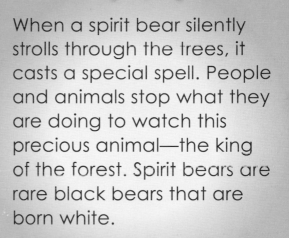

When a spirit bear silently strolls through the trees, it casts a special spell. People and animals stop what they are doing to watch this precious animal—the king of the forest. Spirit bears are rare black bears that are born white.

fairy penguin

Watch this cute little penguin waddle with its pink feet!

Enchanting Stats

Location	Australia and New Zealand
Color	Blue and white
Size	Small
???	Also called the Australian little penguin
⭐⭐⭐	3/5

Fairy penguins are the smallest penguins in the world. They live in burrows by the beach. As the Sun sets, they snuggle up together in their burrows, keeping warm and safe. As the sun rises, they waddle down to the sea to hunt fish and jellyfish to eat.

Reindeer

Listen out for sleighbells—the reindeer are coming!

Enchanting Stats

Location	Arctic
Color	Brown, gray, or white
Size	Large
???	Males and females have antlers
★★★	3/5

44

Reindeer are strong animals that pull sleighs through the snow in the chilly places where they live. Sometimes, reindeer are born all-white, which makes them look even more magical. Some people think they can fly, too! Reindeer are also called caribou.

White Wolf

These magical creatures appear in many fairy tales.

Enchanting Stats

Location	Arctic
Color	White
Size	Medium
???	Eyes appear to glow in the dark
⭐⭐⭐	5/5

46

When wolves appear in fairy tales they are often scary, but real wolves are shy and caring animals. In some stories, white wolves are magical spirits. They are the perfect color for snowy places and their soft fluffy fur keeps them warm on the coldest nights.

Picture Credits

fc= front cover, bc= back cover, t= top, b= bottom, l= left, r= right, c= center

Alamy

8 All Canada Photos, 11tr Nature Photographers Ltd, 13br Juan Aunion, 21br BrazilPhotos, 22 Avalon/Bruce Coleman Inc, 23 BIOSPHOTO, 25 Michael Dwyer, 31 Jeff Milisen, 39tr Stocktrek Images, Inc., 43bl Arco Images GmbH

FLPA

9 Flip Nicklin/Minden Pictures

Getty

17 Sebastian Condrea

Nature Picture Library

9bl Eric Baccega

Shutterstock

Front cover Eric Isselee, front cover bg NYS, 1, 12 Anna Om,2, 23tr Kevin Castaneda, 2-3, 39 GOLFX, 4-5, 35 Keneva Photography, 5tl, 47br Nataliia Melnychuk, 5c, 19br reptiles4all, 5br, 33tl Dennis van de Water, 6 Ste Everington, 7 Dirk van der Heide, 7tr wasilisa, 10 Richard Whitcombe, 11 Vojce, 13 A. Storm Photography, 14 feathercollector, 15 jaja, 16 Kandarp, 17tl Romeo Ninov, 18 Jan Bures, 19 Kurit afshen, 15tr Drakuliren, 20 pranitop, 21 pruit phatsrivong, 24 Iakov Filimonov, 25br Svetlana Timonina, 26 Wicher Bos, 27 Petr Simon, 27tl nattanan726, 28 FotoRequest, 29 RT Images, 29tr Wang LiQiang, 30 S.Rohrlach, 31tl S.Rohrlach, 32 Ritam - Dmitrii Melgunov, 33 Michal Sarauer, 34 Gualberto Becerra, 35bl Fireglo, 36 JodieS, 37 Andrew P. Walmsley, 37bl Chris Watson, 38 MyImages – Micha, 40 NaturesMomentsuk, 41 NaturesMomentsuk, 41tl NaturesMomentsuk, 42 Susan Flashman, 43 oBebee, 44 Roman Roman, 45 Andrew Ivan, 45bl Kertu, 46 Vanucci, 47 Jim Cumming, back cover MAIBYWAY